PLATINUM JUBILEE
COLOURING AND ACTIVITY BOOK

THIS BOOKS BELONGS TO

....

COLOURING

WORDSEARCHES
(AND SOME COLOURING)

PLATINUM JUBILEE 2022

J	Y	P	B	P	J	U	B	I	L	E	E	N	L
B	T	R	R	P	L	A	T	I	N	U	M	C	M
A	S	W	I	H	C	I	O	T	E	T	Z	J	R
M	E	E	T	J	O	T	H	C	R	A	N	O	M
A	J	E	I	K	M	U	L	O	N	D	O	N	H
H	A	T	S	O	M	N	T	E	T	O	R	U	N
G	M	U	H	E	O	I	Y	T	L	A	Y	O	R
N	E	C	H	I	N	B	R	I	T	A	I	N	N
I	L	B	A	N	W	J	L	R	A	R	L	B	H
K	A	M	A	I	E	L	I	Z	A	B	E	T	H
C	M	C	E	A	A	I	E	G	I	I	E	L	L
U	I	O	R	R	L	N	U	L	A	A	G	N	Z
B	L	T	H	O	T	Q	U	E	E	N	H	J	D
A	B	E	I	T	H	N	K	A	U	T	M	O	N

MONARCH
COMMONWEALTH
BUCKINGHAM
JUBILEE
LONDON
ELIZABETH
ROYALTY
BRITISH
QUEEN
PLATINUM
BRITAIN
MAJESTY

THE ROYAL FAMILY

H B N E E E R L E Y J I H A
E T E R H T L T I A A E A B
A D E L L E T E T E M K M E
N N W B O L I E S M E M E A
D M R A A U I N L E S E G T
R A R R R Z I C E R S C H R
E I H A H D I S H G A E A I
W L K A T E L L D A U H N C
A L A E U E A I E D R E C E
N I T E Y R I T L T K L I A
E W E W R H A H W I B D E E
E G E O R G E H C E B B G S
L A U E A M L N L R H E B L
T A B O H C S E I E A W T G

KATE
EUGENIE
CHARLES
CHARLETTE
LOUIS
ELIZABETH
BEATRICE
ARCHIE
MEGHAN
WILLIAM
JAMES
HARRY
LILIBET
GEORGE
ANDREW
EDWARD

ROYAL PALACES

B	E	N	E	O	T	K	H	K	A	N	I	K	E
N	T	A	R	E	T	S	N	I	M	T	S	E	W
O	B	N	N	T	E	R	E	K	H	S	N	E	I
D	M	T	Q	C	T	N	A	D	I	T	I	M	N
N	W	T	T	E	N	N	C	S	G	J	R	A	D
O	H	P	T	K	N	D	N	G	E	A	N	H	S
L	I	E	L	A	M	B	E	T	H	M	W	G	O
F	T	L	W	N	Q	A	W	N	H	E	T	N	R
O	E	I	N	T	R	O	T	O	K	S	I	I	C
R	H	K	E	N	S	I	N	G	T	O	N	K	A
E	A	O	E	W	H	A	M	P	T	O	N	C	S
W	L	E	H	H	C	M	K	C	C	U	K	U	T
O	L	W	B	M	O	L	F	A	A	W	N	B	L
T	B	A	N	Q	U	E	T	I	N	G	W	L	E

STJAMES
KENSINGTON
WINDSORCASTLE
WHITEHALL
WESTMINSTER
TOWEROFLONDON
LAMBETH
BUCKINGHAM
BANQUETING
KEW
HAMPTON

CONNECT THE DOTS

(AND SOME COLOURING)

ROYAL CROWN
CONNECT THE DOTS

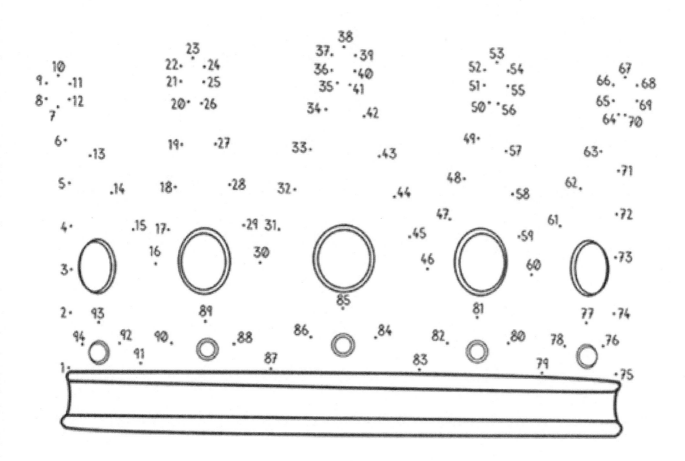

ROYAL CROWN 2
CONNECT THE DOTS

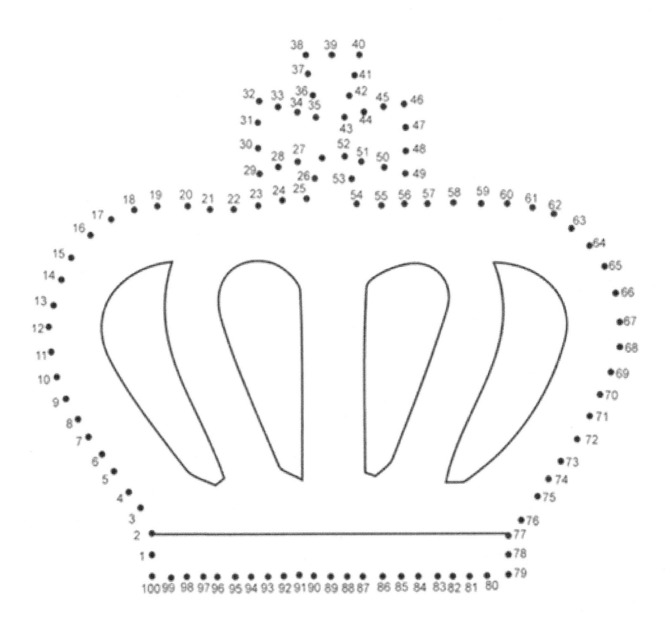

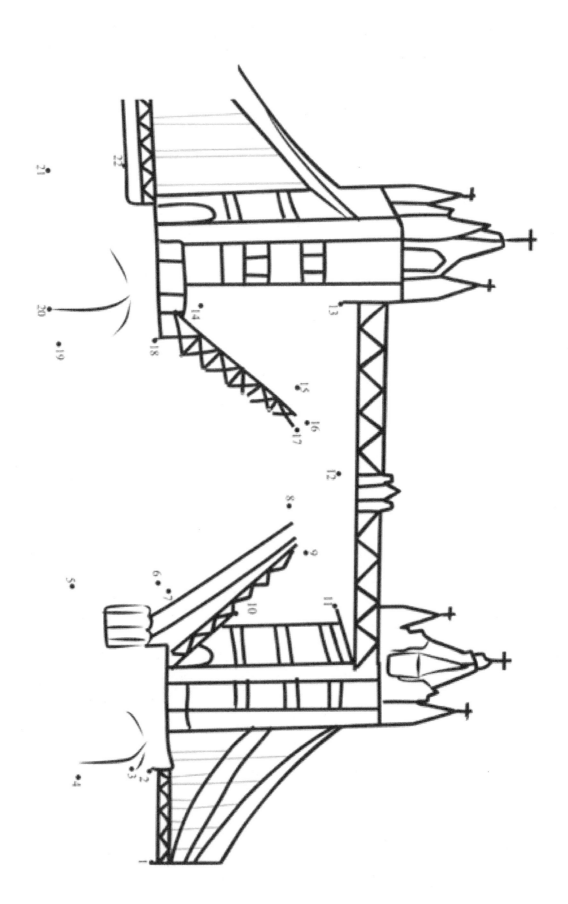

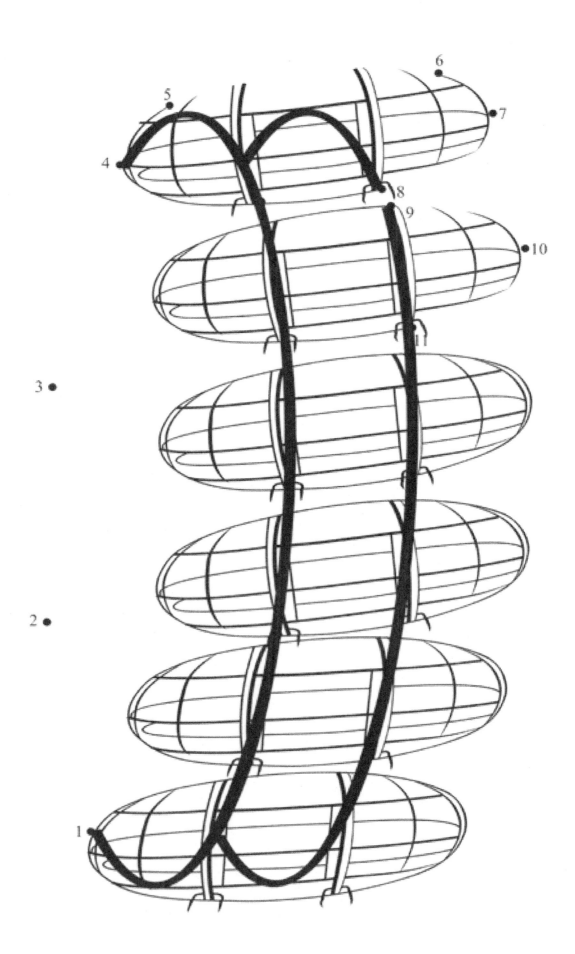

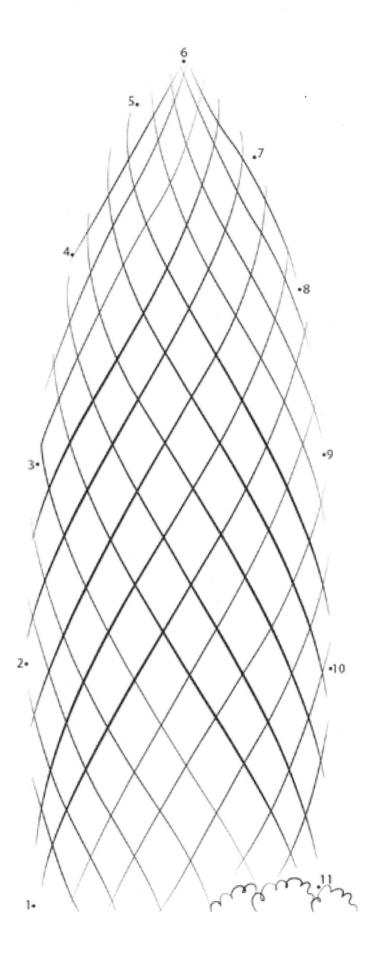

HANDWRITING

Buckingham

Buckingham

Buckingham

Buckingham

Buckingham

Buckingham

Elizabeth II

Elizabeth II

Elizabeth II

Elizabeth II

Elizabeth II

Elizabeth II

Britain

Britain

Britain

Britain

Britain

Britain

Platinum

Platinum

Platinum

Platinum

Platinum

Platinum

Jubilee

Jubilee

Jubilee

Jubilee

Jubilee

Jubilee

Corgi

Corgi

Corgi

Corgi

Corgi

Corgi

Royalty

Royalty

Royalty

Royalty

Royalty

Royalty

COLOURING

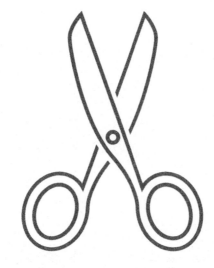

CUTTING OUT
(AND SOME COLOURING)

CREATE YOUR OWN BOOKMARKS!

CREATE YOUR OWN FLAG!

FUN FACTS!
QUEEN ELIZABETH II

Did You Know...

- Queen Elizabeth II was born in a Townhouse in London

- She was the first female member of the royal family to become a full-time active member of the British Armed Forces.

- She promised to devote her life to public service on her 21st birthday.

- She received more than 2,500 wedding gifts when she married Prince Philip, Duke of Edinburgh, in 1947.

- She was the first monarch to be crowned in a televised coronation ceremony.

- She was the first monarch to open Parliament in Canada.

- She has owned more than 30 corgis over the course of her lifetime.

- She is Head of a Commonwealth of 54 nations.

- She is the most well travelled monarch in history.

- She is the longest reigning monarch in British and Commonwealth history.

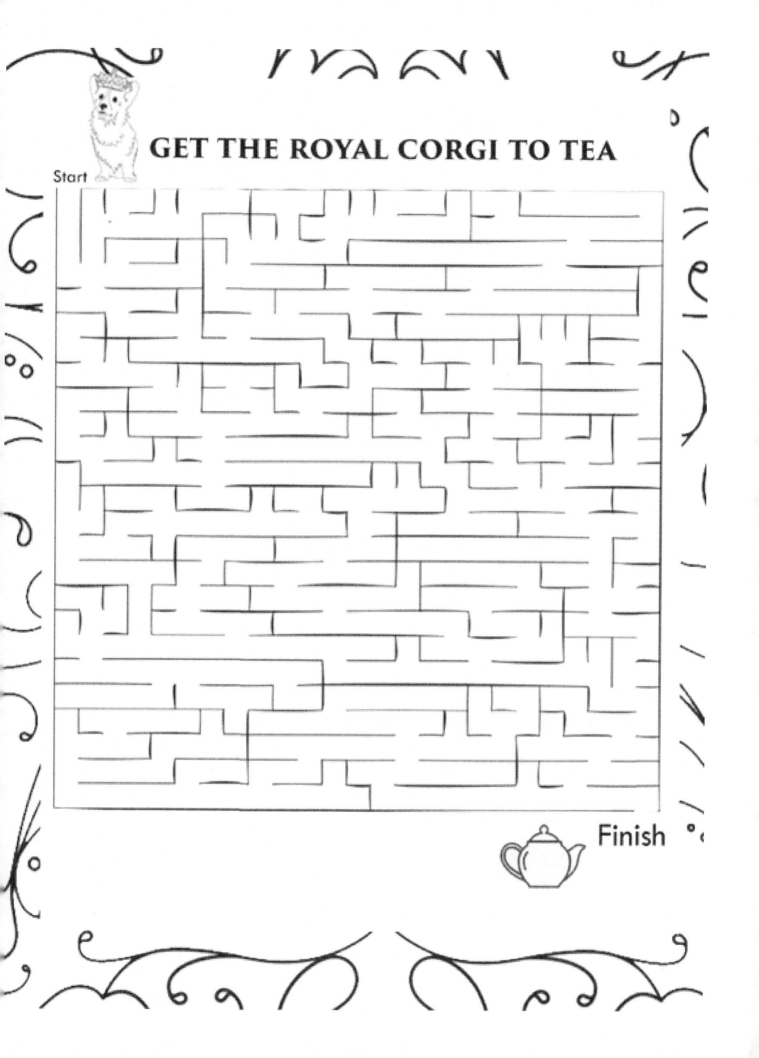

GET THE ROYAL CORGI TO TEA

Start

Finish

HELP THE BUS GET TO BUCKINGHAM PALACE

HELP THE GUARD GET TO THE X

COLOURING

PLATINUM

JUBILEE

Platinum Jubilee 2022

SPOT THE DIFFERENCE

(AND SOME COLOURING)

 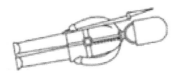 

 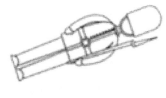 

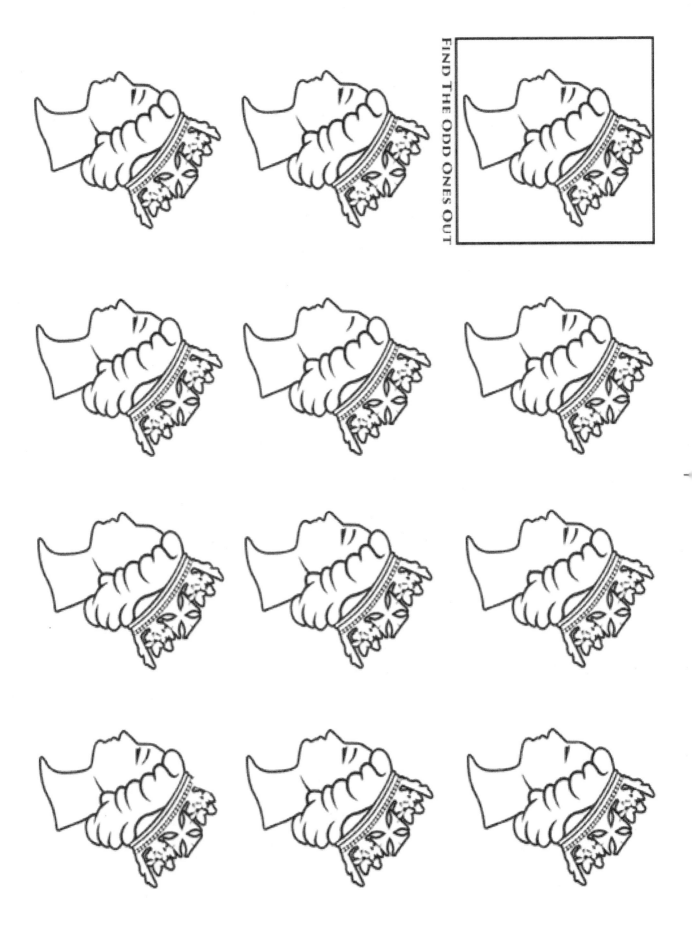

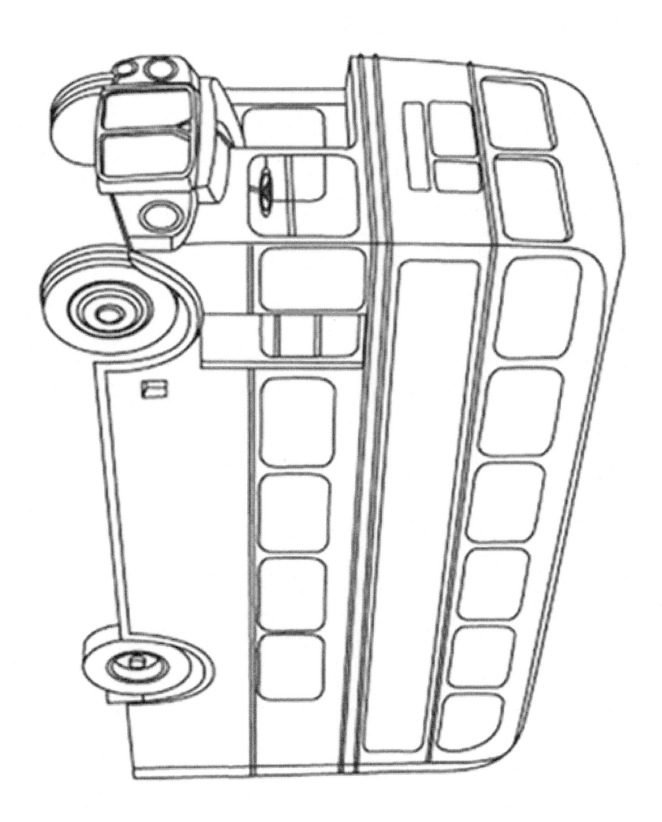

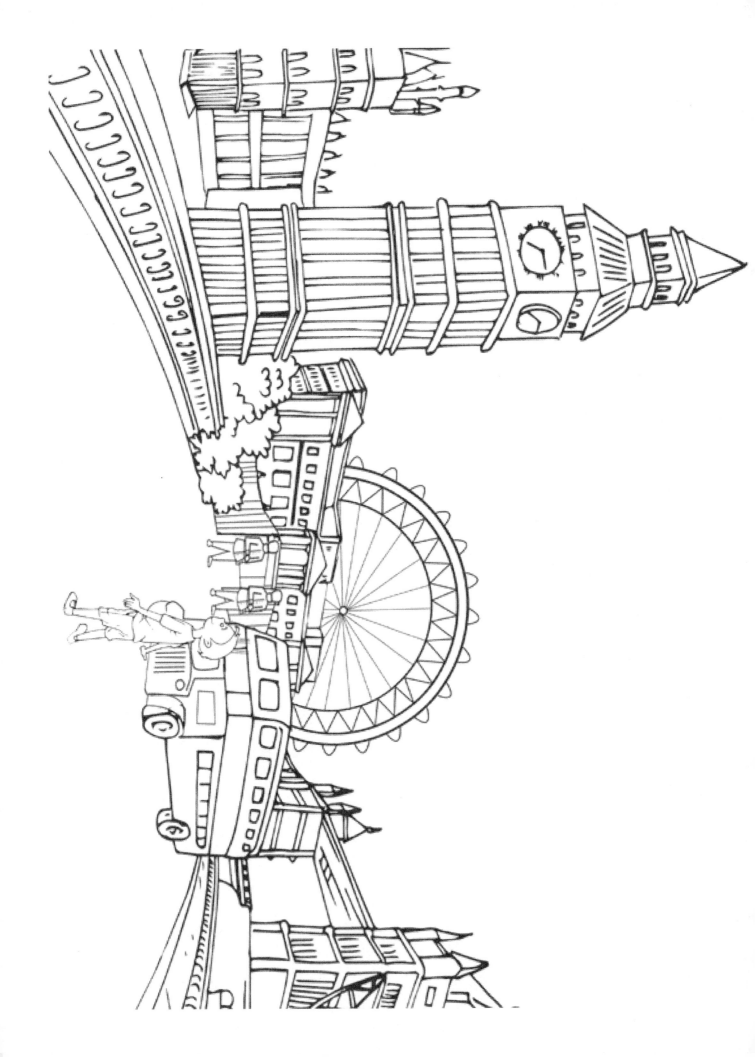

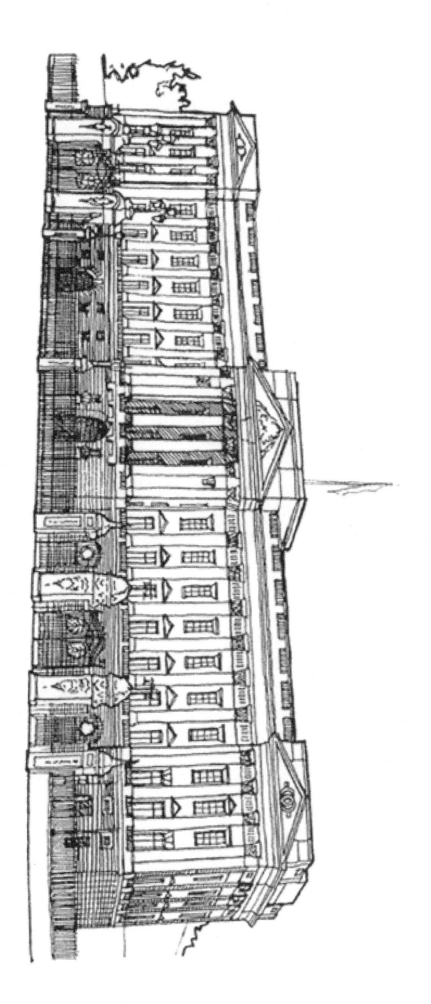

BUCKINGHAM PALACE

COLOURING

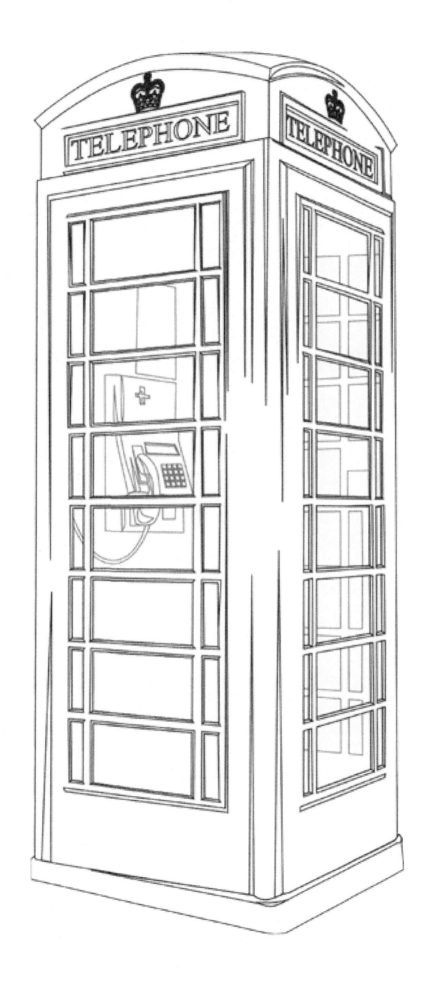

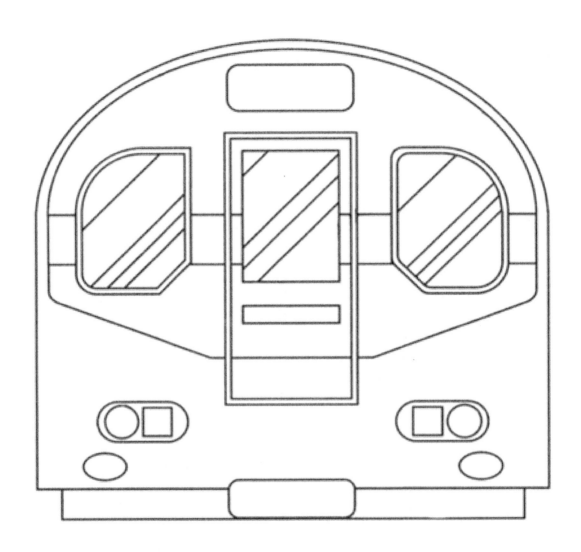

PLATINUM JUBILEE
COLOURING AND ACTIVITY BOOK

Printed in Great Britain
by Amazon